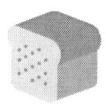

Sourdough Chronicles From Starter to Artisan

The secrets course ofourdough step by step to make creations with incredible flavors, fragrances and appearance.

Massimo Parrucci

Dedication

-to all my mistakes-

This collection embodies the culmination of extensive collaboration and research with Italy's finest chefs and master bakers. It aims to share the knowledge and secrets of an Italian baking tradition that has been passed down through generations.

PREFACE

Kneading is a ritual, a dance of gestures and precisely calibrated movements. It's a process that takes simple ingredients and, with slow and rhythmic finesse, transforms them into something new and alive: a magnificent dough, intricate yet perfectly balanced. Making bread is both a physical and spiritual journey. It teaches us about boundaries and patience.

Throughout the preparation, we learn to tune in to the subtle cues: the dough as it rises, the bread as it bakes and turns a golden hue.
It's a world unto itself, filled with distinct shapes, scents, tastes, and colors.
Crafting a dough is also a lesson in introspection, guiding us to observe and better ourselves.

Making bread is an embrace of the joy found in giving to others. To share a piece of your own sourdough is to seek nothing more than a smile in return.

PASTING

When we talk about flour, perhaps many of you first think of the classic wheat flour 0. But in reality, any milled flour obtained from a dry ingredient, can be considered as such as, for example, the flour of
rice, peas, chestnuts, carrots, chickpeas, etc.
In these pages, we will elaborate on flours made from wheat.
These flours are divided into two major types:
Soft wheat flours and durum wheat flours, also called semolina.

The difference between the 2 types lies in the raw material used.

These flours are made from different types of wheat; soft wheat flours are made from soft wheat, and durum wheat flours are made from hard wheat.

When discussing flour, many might first think of the classic all-purpose flour, a staple in American kitchens. But just as in Italy, where you have the wheat flour 0, there's a vast array of flours derived from various dry ingredients, such as rice, peas, chestnuts, carrots, and chickpeas. In this section, we'll delve into flours primarily made from wheat.

These flours are categorized into two main types: Soft wheat flours and durum wheat flours, often referred to as semolina.

The distinction between these two lies in the raw materials used. They're derived from different wheat varieties; soft wheat flours come from soft wheat, while durum wheat flours are produced from hard wheat.

SOFT WHEAT FLOURS (With USA Equivalents)

- **Farina 00 (Italy)**: In the USA, this is closely related to **Cake Flour or Pastry Flour**. It's the most refined wheat flour, with a minimal bran content and a higher endosperm percentage. Ideal for cakes, cookies, pizzas, and focaccias that require short leavening times.

- **Farina 0 (Italy)**: This aligns with the **Bread Flour** commonly used in the USA. It's richer in gluten, making it the go-to choice for bread, pizza, and other baked goods that benefit from a chewier texture.

- **Farina Tipo 1 (Italy)**: This can be likened to **High Gluten Flour** in the USA. With an increased bran and protein content, it's versatile, suitable for crumbly cakes as well as breads that need longer leavening.

- **Farina Tipo 2 (Italy)**: This is somewhat akin to the **Whole Wheat Flour** found in the USA, but it's less refined. It's the choice for those aiming for a more rustic touch in their baked creations.

- **Whole Wheat Flour (Italy)**: This matches the **Whole Grain Flour** in the USA. It stands out nutritionally, encompassing the entire grain - bran, germ, and endosperm.

- **Manitoba Flour (Italy)**: This is what Americans would recognize as **High Protein Bread Flour or Strong Bread Flour**. It shines when used in recipes requiring extended leavening times, like bread and brioches.

HARD WHEAT (With USA Equivalents)

Durum wheat flours, or semolina, are distinct from regular flours. They have a coarser texture and a higher protein content compared to the Italian type 00 flour. Doughs made with durum wheat semolina are less stretchy, making them less elastic but much more robust. This characteristic makes these flours ideal for certain types of bread, like Altamura bread, or for making fresh or dried pasta.

Here are the four primary types of durum wheat semolina:

- **Semola di Grano Duro (Italy)**: In the USA, this is simply known as **Semolina**. It's slightly grainy, resembling fine sand with a pale-yellow hue. It's the top choice for making fresh or dried pasta and specific desserts.

- **Semolato di Grano Duro (Italy)**: This doesn't have a direct equivalent in the USA but can be likened to a **Coarser Semolina**. It's used similarly to Semola di Grano Duro.

- **Semola Integrale di Grano Duro (Italy)**: This corresponds to **Whole Grain Semolina** in the USA. It's akin to regular semolina but is whole grain, making it nutritionally richer.

- **Semolino di Grano Duro (Italy)**: This is similar to **Fine Semolina or Durum Flour** in the USA. It's a very finely milled semolina, perfect for fresh or dried pasta, various bread types, and specific desserts.

In summary, while Italy boasts a rich variety of wheat flours, each with its unique characteristics, the USA has its counterparts. Whether it's the refined Farina 00 or the robust Manitoba flour, there's an American equivalent that can be used to achieve similar culinary results.

THE POWER OF FLOUR

When discussing flour, terms like "strong" or "weak" often come up. But what do they mean?

In Italy, **00 flour** (Cake Flour) is considered very weak. This type of flour can't absorb much water, making it unsuitable for long fermentation processes. It's perfect for making fresh egg pasta, shortcrust pastry, or cookies.

On the other hand, **Manitoba flour** (Bread Flour) is very strong, suitable for breads and other baked goods that require long fermentation. The strength of a flour is determined by its protein content, specifically gluten. Gluten gives elasticity to the dough, and a flour with low gluten content will not be very elastic and won't be suitable for doughs with high hydration.

So, how can you differentiate between a strong and a weak flour? The strength of flour is indicated by the parameter W, followed by a number. For instance, 00 flours are very weak with a W170, medium flours used for pizza have W240-260, while very strong ones are around W400.

Gluten is the protein component of dough. It's a combination of two proteins and water. The development of gluten is influenced by:

- **Mechanical work**: Kneading, whether by hand or with a mixer.

- **Timing**: Allowing the right amount of time for gluten formation.

- **Temperature**: Heat aids in gluten formation.

In summary, there's a wide variety of white flours, each with its unique properties. It's crucial to select the right flour based on the intended preparation. For instance, for making pizza, a medium strength W240 flour is ideal. Using a flour that's too weak or too strong can result in undesirable dough characteristics.

Water plays a pivotal role in dough preparation. While many focus on the quality of flour, salt, or oil, the quality of water is often overlooked. The hardness of water, which indicates the presence of mineral salts, can significantly impact the dough.

Water hardness is measured in French degrees (F°). Soft water has a value of less than 5 F°, moderate hardness ranges between 6 - 20 F°, and anything above 20 F° is considered hard.

Why is this important? The ideal water for dough preparation should have moderate hardness. Soft water can produce a sticky dough with a weak gluten network. On the other hand, very hard water can slow down yeast activity and fermentation due to its strong gluten network.

For optimal results, water with a hardness between 12 and 18 degrees (within the moderate range) should be used. This ensures an ideal pH for the mix, resulting in a balanced gluten network that allows for successful yeast development and fermentation.

The Basics: Leavening and Maturation

In the world of baking, two essential processes shape the transformation of dough: leavening and maturation. While leavening is a concept familiar to many, maturation holds equal importance, albeit less recognized.

Leavening is a swift process. It kicks off almost immediately, often within just 2 hours of starting the dough preparation.

However, within this short span, the dough doesn't get an opportunity to mature sufficiently. For proper maturation, the dough needs to rest for at least 24-30 hours. When yeast is added to the dough, it consumes the dough's components and releases carbon dioxide. This gas gets trapped within the gluten network formed during kneading, resulting in a dough with well-defined air pockets or alveoli.

On the other hand, **maturation** involves the breakdown of complex molecules into simpler ones.

These simpler molecules are easier to digest, ensuring that a well-matured dough won't leave you feeling heavy after consumption. To harmonize the processes of leavening and maturation, it's beneficial to slow down the leavening.

This can be achieved using a refrigerator. At temperatures of 4-8°C (39-46°F), the refrigerator allows the dough to develop over two days, ensuring both adequate leavening and maturation.

Direct, Semi-Direct, and Indirect

In the vast world of leavened products, dough can be categorized into three primary types based on their kneading process: direct, semi-direct, and indirect. The distinction among these primarily lies in their method of processing.

Direct Dough

In this straightforward method, all ingredients - water, flour, salt, yeast, oil, and others - are combined in a single phase.

Advantages:

- **Simplicity:** Just mix all the ingredients, and you're set to start the leavening process. It's the most practical method as it doesn't involve multiple steps.

Disadvantages:

- **Limited Flavor Profile:** Direct doughs tend to have less depth in flavors and aromas. However, the controlled direct dough method, which allows the dough to rise and mature in the refrigerator, compensates for these shortcomings by enhancing the flavor and aroma.

Semi-Direct Dough

This method involves mixing all the ingredients in one go and then incorporating a "carryover" dough. This dough, prepared in advance and set aside, kickstarts the maturation process. When added to a new batch, it infuses the mixture with additional flavors and aromas. However, its exact impact on the new batch's leavening is hard to quantify, leading to potential inconsistencies during extended rising periods.

Indirect Dough

Distinguished by its multiple processing steps, indirect dough is primarily used for bread-making. It imparts unique flavors, aromas, and offers a longer shelf life.

The two main categories within indirect dough are:

- **Biga:** A compact dough with hydration levels between 45% and 50%. It's left to rise for 16 to 48 hours. The flour used varies in strength based on the rising duration.

- **Poolish:** A 100% hydration dough, it's made with equal parts flour and water, along with yeast. The quantity of yeast varies based on the leavening duration, ranging from 4 to 16-18 hours.

While both Biga and Poolish offer exceptional flavors, aromas, and digestibility, they are complex and might be challenging for beginners.

As you continue your journey in the world of baking, understanding these kneading methods will empower you to choose the best technique for your desired outcome. Happy baking!

The Art of Kneading

Kneading, a fundamental step in the baking process, plays a pivotal role in determining the texture, elasticity, and strength of the dough. It's not just about mixing the ingredients; it's about understanding the science behind it and using the right techniques to achieve the desired outcome.

Stringing vs. Folding

At the heart of kneading lies the distinction between stringing and folding.

- **Stringing**: This technique focuses on enhancing the dough's strength, especially during its rising and spreading phases. By stringing the dough, we create a firm and rigid mesh that effectively traps gases, ensuring the dough rises well. This strength is crucial, especially when the dough is under stress.

- **Elasticity**: A key attribute of a well-kneaded dough is its elasticity. Without it, rolling out certain baked goods, like pizza, becomes a challenge. The elasticity is not inherent but is imparted through the manipulation technique employed during kneading.

The Role of Folds

While stringing imparts strength, folding gives the dough its much-needed structure.

- **Purpose of Folds**: Contrary to popular belief, folds are not primarily used to give the dough its stringiness. Instead, they contribute to the formation of the glutinous mesh, providing the dough with structure. A dough can be perfectly strung, but without the right structure, it won't achieve the desired consistency.

- **Achieving Structure**: Consider a freshly kneaded dough made from the right ingredients. It might have the perfect consistency, but it lacks structure. This is where folding comes into play. By incorporating folds, we give the dough its actual strength, transforming it into a solid, robust mass.

In Conclusion

Kneading is not just a mechanical process; it's an art. By understanding the nuances of stringing and folding, and by employing the right techniques, one can master the art of kneading, producing dough that is both strong and elastic, ready to be transformed into delicious baked goods.

Understanding Autolysis

Autolysis, derived from the Greek words 'auto' (self) and 'lysis' (splitting), is a technique in bread-making that involves allowing a mixture of flour and water to rest, facilitating the development of gluten and enhancing the dough's extensibility.

The Autolysis Process

1. **Initiation**: Begin by sifting the desired flour(s) into a bowl. Carefully stir and introduce about 55% of the recipe's water. Note that the percentage can vary based on the type of flour. For instance, whole wheat flour tends to absorb more water than white flour.

2. **Mixing**: At this juncture, there's no need for rigorous kneading. The goal is to ensure the flour is well-moistened, forming damp clumps. It's crucial to ensure no dry flour remains at the bowl's bottom, as this can lead to undesirable lumps in the dough.

3. **Resting**: Once the flour is uniformly wet, cover the mixture and let it rest for the duration specified in the recipe.

Autolysis vs. Biga

It's essential to differentiate between autolysis and biga. While both are pre-fermentation techniques:

- **Autolysis**: Involves only water and flour. It's typically employed when dealing with highly hydrated doughs, making the subsequent kneading process more manageable.

- **Biga or Poolish**: These are pre-ferments that include flour, water, and yeast, serving as a starter for the main dough.

Benefits of Autolysis

- **Gluten Development**: Autolysis aids in the early formation of the gluten network. When you return to the dough after the autolytic rest, you'll find the gluten partially developed, making the addition of other ingredients and kneading more straightforward.

- **Handling Hydrated Dough**: For recipes demanding high hydration (70-80%), autolysis simplifies the process. By introducing water in stages, the dough becomes more manageable.

- **Optimal Gluten Mesh**: Autolysis not only accelerates gluten development but also refines its quality. This impacts the bread's alveolation, resulting in a softer crumb and better growth.

Practical Tips

- **Timing**: Aim for an autolytic rest of at least 40 minutes, though 1-2 hours is ideal.

- **Temperature**: In summer, consider refrigerating the autolytic mixture to maintain a cooler dough temperature. In contrast, during winter, a dish towel covering at room temperature suffices.

In Essence

Autolysis is a technique that harnesses the natural processes within flour. By promoting cellular self-disintegration and fermentation, it breaks down proteins, releases sugars, and fosters gluten formation. While not mandatory, it's a method that can elevate the quality of your bread, making it a worthy addition to any baker's repertoire.

MOTHER YEAST

The Ubiquitous Yeast

Yeast, a single-celled fungus, is omnipresent. From the air we breathe to the very skin we inhabit, yeast plays a silent yet significant role in our environment. While some strains can cause diseases or spoil food, others are invaluable in culinary arts, particularly in bread-making, brewing, and winemaking.

The Yeast's Role in Leavening

At the heart of the leavening process, yeast consumes sugars and bacteria, undergoing metabolism. This process yields energy, alcohol, and carbon dioxide. In the culinary world, the carbon dioxide aids in leavening, while alcohol finds its place in beverages like beer and wine.

Types of Leavening

1. **Physical Leavening (Mechanical Leavening):**

   o   This isn't true leavening but a result of thermal expansion during baking.

   o   Examples include sponge cakes with whipped egg whites and puff pastries. In the latter, alternating layers of fat and dough create water vapor during baking, leading to the pastry's distinct layers.

2. **Chemical Leavening**:

   o Common in pastries and homemade cakes.

   o Instant chemical yeast, activated by heat, is the primary agent. It releases carbon dioxide during baking, causing the dough to rise.

   o This yeast, a white powder, comprises sodium bicarbonate and an acidic component.

   o Homemade chemical yeast can be crafted by combining cream of tartar, baking soda, and cornstarch.

   o

3. **Organic Leavening (Fermentation)**:

   o This natural process involves live yeasts consuming dough sugars, producing carbon dioxide, which gives rise to the characteristic bubbles in products like pizza.

   o Types of yeast for organic leavening include:

     ▪ Fresh brewer's yeast (ball-like appearance)

     ▪ Dry brewer's yeast (resembling light brown grains)

     ▪ Mother yeast (dough-like consistency)

   o Ideal for long-rise baked goods such as brioche, jam croissants, white bread, and pizza dough. These require extended leavening periods before baking.

In Conclusion

Leavening is a fascinating blend of science and art, transforming simple ingredients into culinary masterpieces. Whether it's the light fluffiness of a cake, the layered richness of a croissant, or the chewy delight of a pizza, the magic of leavening is evident in every bite.

Sourdough: The Magical Creature of the Kitchen

Sourdough is often referred to as a "magical creature" of the kitchen, sparking intrigue and wonder among the less experienced. From those completely unfamiliar with it to those who cherish and protect it in a jar, often speaking to it affectionately as one would to a beloved pet, sourdough holds a special place in many hearts. This guide aims to provide comprehensive information about sourdough, catering to both newcomers and seasoned enthusiasts.

The Basics of Sourdough

At its core, sourdough consists of just two ingredients: water and flour. When allowed to mature, the ambient yeasts and bacteria present in the air and flour initiate the fermentation process. The primary challenge with sourdough is its maintenance, which necessitates regular "refreshments" to keep the fermentation active and sustain its life cycle.

Initiating the Sourdough Process

Every environment contains bacteria and yeasts. By simply mixing flour and water, one can kickstart the creation of sourdough. To expedite the fermentation, a starter can be introduced, such as ripe fruit puree, yogurt, or honey.

Contrary to brewer's yeast, which contains a specific strain of microorganisms, sourdough is home to a diverse array of yeasts and bacteria. The lactic fermentation produces organic acids, enhancing flavors and aromas while facilitating the development of air pockets in the dough. The ideal pH for sourdough hovers around 4.5. While commonly used for pizza, focaccia, and bread, sourdough is also suitable for more intricate recipes like pandoro and panettone.

Types of Sourdough Starters

There are primarily two versions of sourdough starters, differentiated by their hydration levels:

Liquid Sourdough (Lycoli):

- Prepared with equal parts of water and flour.

- Produces small air pockets, imparting elasticity to the dough.

- Has a sharp taste due to the presence of alcohol and acetic acid.

- Enhances bread crust and strengthens weaker cereal proteins, such as rye.

- Can be stored in an airtight jar in the refrigerator for up to 4 days.

Solid Sourdough:

- Requires less water compared to flour (approximately 50%).

- Features a robust structure with coarse, irregular air pockets, ensuring a strong rise.

- Results in a soft and aromatic crumb, courtesy of the lactic acid produced during fermentation.

- Ideal for recipes that demand precise processing, aiding in gluten layering.

- Refreshment involves using, for instance, 100 grams of dough, adding an equal amount of flour, and half the quantity of water. The dough should be mixed until soft and cohesive, and refreshed at least every 48 hours.

In conclusion, sourdough is a testament to the wonders of nature and fermentation. With dedication, care, and a touch of magic, it can be harnessed to produce baking masterpieces.

PREPARATION (solid sourdough and liquid sourdough)

Solid Sourdough: Solid sourdough is a blend of flour and water, acidified by the growth of microorganisms, enabling the natural fermentation of the mixture.

This yeast is more digestible than others, has a long shelf life, and ensures excellent leavening. Crafting it at home is straightforward but demands meticulous steps and patience.

Ingredients:

- 200 g of 0 flour (approximately 1.5 cups)
- 100 ml of lukewarm water (about 0.5 cups)
- A tablespoon of honey

Tip: For sourdough preparation, opt for chlorine-free water. Chlorine can hinder the yeast's structure. Always use natural mineral water with a low fixed residue for both preparation and refreshments.

Procedure:

1. Pour the flour into a bowl and gradually add water.
2. Stir the mixture with a spoon, following the bowl's edges, until a smooth consistency is achieved.
3. Knead the dough on a work surface until it's non-sticky.

4. Transfer it to a glass jar, make a cross cut on its top surface, and cover with perforated plastic wrap.

5. Allow the dough to rest in a dry, clean place for 48 hours. The oxygen will facilitate bacteria to feed on the yeast, initiating the fermentation process. After 48 hours, the dough will start to rise, forming alveoli.

6. Refreshments can now commence.

Liquid Sourdough (Licoli): Just like solid sourdough, it's crucial to use organic, preferably stone-ground flour and chlorine-free mineral water for licoli. Utilize a cylindrical glass jar for storage.

Procedure:

1. On Day 1 at 9:00 am, mix 100 g of organic flour with 100 g of water at 29/30°C (86°F) in a bowl. Ensure a smooth, lump-free cream.

2. Transfer the cream to the jar and cover with sterile gauze. Let it rest at room temperature in a dry place for 24 hours.

3. On Day 2 at 9:00 am, if the dough has doubled or multiplied its volume and emits a strong acidic odor, it's on the right track. Take 100 g of the cream, discard the rest, and mix with 100 g of organic flour and 100 g of water at 29/30°C (86°F). Place the mixture in a clean jar, cover with gauze, and let it rest for another 24 hours.

4. Continue this process, observing the growth and smell of the licoli. By Day 5, after the first refreshment, the licoli should be ready for storage in the refrigerator. The remaining 200 g can be used for dough preparation, which will double in size in 6-8 hours.

Tip: A newborn yeast requires about 15 to 20 days to fully mature. From Day 6 to Day 13, regular refreshments are essential to empower the growing yeast. Refresh every 4 days to maintain its activity, storing it in the fridge.

Final Notes: Sourdough, whether liquid or solid, is ripe for baking when it has doubled in volume post-refreshment. To track this doubling, mark the yeast level in the jar. Once it doubles, it's baking-ready.

The leftover sourdough, previously discarded, can now be used to whip up delicious treats. This residue, now termed "excess," can be transformed into delightful recipes, which will be discussed in subsequent chapters.

Always be vigilant for mold. If mold appears, it indicates an error in the process.

In such cases, discard the entire batch and start anew.

Solid Sourdough:

- **Definition:** A mixture of flour and water, acidified by the growth of microorganisms, facilitating natural fermentation.

- **Advantages:** It's more digestible than other yeasts, has a longer shelf life, and ensures superior leavening.

Ingredients for Preparation:

- **Flour:** 200g of 0 flour (equivalent to one and a half cup).

- **Water:** 100ml of lukewarm water (half cup).

- **Sweetener:** A tablespoon of honey for added flavor and to aid fermentation.

Preparation Process:

- **Mixing:** Gradually add water to the flour in a bowl. Achieve a smooth consistency by shaping the dough with a spoon.

- **Kneading:** Transfer the dough to a work surface and knead until it's no longer sticky.

- **Storage:** Place the dough in a glass jar, score the top with a cross-cut, and cover with perforated plastic wrap.

- **Resting:** Allow the dough to rest for 48 hours in a dry, clean place. This resting period lets oxygen enter, which bacteria use to feed on the yeast, initiating fermentation. After 48 hours, the dough will start to rise, forming alveoli or air pockets.

Refreshment:

- **Initial Step:** Remove the top part of the dough, which would have become harder.

- **Refreshing:** Take 100g from the inside of the dough, place it in a bowl, and add equal parts of flour and half the amount of water. This process rejuvenates the yeast and is crucial for maintaining its vitality.

Temperature Considerations: If the sourdough is stored in the refrigerator, it's essential to bring it to room temperature before any refreshment. This might take longer in colder seasons.

Refreshment Process: Removing the Hardened Part: The top part of the yeast, which has been exposed to air, needs to be removed before refreshing.

Calculating the Amount for Refreshment: For a recipe requiring 150g of yeast, divide the amount by 5 to determine the water weight. Multiply the water weight by 2 to get the combined weight of flour and yeast.

Methods of Incorporating Sourdough in Recipes:

- **Dissolution:** Dissolve the sourdough in water and then add it to the batter.

- **Direct Mixing:** Add water to the batter, cut the sourdough into pieces, and mix it in. Using honey or a bit of sugar can aid the leavening process as sugars feed the yeast.

Conservation of Sourdough: Traditional Milanese Refreshment: Ideal for making large leavened items like pandoro and panettone. This method creates a rigid and compact gluten mesh, making it unsuitable for bread or pizza. This refreshment uses a 1:1 ratio, adding an equal quantity of flour to the sourdough. The refreshment should be done every 24/48 hours.

Recovery Techniques:

- **Acidic Dough:** If the pH of the sourdough falls below 4.2, it becomes too acidic. This can be identified by a strong vinegar smell and a grayish, sticky appearance. Such dough needs to be refreshed using specific steps.

- **Strong Dough:** A strong sourdough is darker with visible spherical alveoli. If it's too strong, it needs to be soaked in water.

- **Weak Dough:** A weak sourdough is stiff with no internal air pockets. It requires a specific refreshment process.

Sourdough is a living entity, and like all living things, it requires care and attention. The process of preparing, using, and conserving sourdough is both a science and an art. While the steps might seem intricate, with dedication, patience, and a passion for baking, one can master the technique and create delectable baked goods. Remember, every baker has their journey, filled with trials, errors, and successes. Embrace the process, learn from each experience, and enjoy the art of baking with sourdough.

BREAD

In the heart of every kitchen, there's a story of bread. It's a tale as old as time, woven through the fabric of countless cultures and civilizations. The pandemic, with its challenges and introspections, saw many of us returning to this age-old tradition, finding comfort in the rhythmic dance of kneading and the warm embrace of a freshly baked loaf.

When you decide to make bread by hand, you're not just mixing flour and water. You're pouring in memories, patience, and a sprinkle of love. Perhaps it's a rebellion against the store-bought loaves that harden too soon or lack the authentic taste of home. Or maybe it's the joy of having a bread that stays fresh for a week, a testament to your effort and care.

But beyond the taste and longevity, making bread is a communal act. It's an opportunity to gather around the table, to share stories and laughter, to teach and to learn. It's a moment to pause and appreciate the simple ingredients that, when combined, create magic. Water, flour, and a starter - be it the bubbling sourdough or the trusty yeast - come together in a symphony of flavors and textures.

The choice of flour is a chapter in itself. Opting for type 2 or whole wheat flour is like choosing the scenic route for a journey. These flours, rich in fibers and minerals, offer a depth of flavor and a treasure trove of nutrients. They stand in stark contrast to the refined landscapes of 00 flour, bringing rustic charm and wholesome goodness to every bite.

Sourdough enthusiasts will vouch for its gentle nature. While commercial breads might weigh you down, sourdough, with its long fermentation, is like a soft lullaby for the stomach. It's a reminder that sometimes, slowing down and taking our time can lead to the best results.

But at its core, bread-making is a celebration. It's a dance of the senses, from the silky touch of dough to the golden hues of a crusty loaf. It's the pride in creating, the joy in sharing, and the love in savoring. It's a nod to the Mediterranean traditions, where bread graces every table, and every meal is a feast.

So, as we embark on this bread-making adventure, let's cherish the journey as much as the destination. Let's celebrate the stories, the traditions, and the hands that have kneaded before us. For in every loaf, there's a world waiting to be discovered.

Classic Italian bread

Ah, the timeless allure of freshly baked bread. This classic Italian bread recipe takes us on a nostalgic journey back to the days when our grandmothers lovingly crafted each loaf by hand. Imagine a bread that's soft and tender on the inside, but on the outside? A golden, crunchy crust that beckons.

Details:

- **Servings:** 8

- **Preparation Time:** 30 minutes

- **Baking Time:** 25 minutes

Ingredients:

- 100g (3.5 oz) refreshed sourdough starter

- 500g (4 cups) type 0 flour (akin to American all-purpose flour)

- 300g (1 1/4 cups) water

- Salt, to taste

- A generous drizzle of extra virgin olive oil

Steps to Bread Perfection:

1. Begin with the sourdough starter. Mix it into warm water and let it sit for about 5 minutes. Give it a good stir using a wooden spoon.

2. In a large mixing bowl, combine the flour, olive oil, and salt. Now, introduce the sourdough mixture and knead until you've got a smooth, unified dough.

3. Cover your dough with plastic wrap. Let it rest and dream for 24 hours. If it's winter, a turned-off oven is its cozy bed. In summer, tuck it into the fridge.

4. Day 2: Your dough should've grown impressively, nearly tripling in size. Spread it out on a floured surface, shaping it into a rectangle.

5. Fold the long sides of the rectangle towards the center. Then, do the same with the shorter sides.

6. Embrace the "pirlatura" technique. It's a fancy Italian term for rounding out the dough by spinning it with floured hands. Think of it as giving your dough a mini dance lesson.

7. Once you've achieved a nice round shape, place the dough in a basket lined with a clean cloth. Sprinkle some flour on top and let it rise until it doubles in size (about 3-4 hours).

8. Gently transfer the risen dough onto a baking sheet lined with parchment paper. Dust it with flour.

9. With a sharp knife, make some artistic incisions on the bread's surface. Bake in a preheated oven at 428°F (220°C) for about 20-25 minutes.

10. And voilà! Your homemade sourdough bread is ready to impress. Serve it warm for that extra touch of magic.

Pro Tip: For an even crunchier crust, activate your oven's steam function or place a bowl of water inside during baking. Another popular method is to brush the bread's surface with a saltwater brine in the last 20 seconds of baking.

Enjoy the fruits of your labor and the rich tradition of Italian baking!

There's something truly magical about baking bread at home. The aroma, the warm slices fresh out of the oven, and the knowledge that you've created something wholesome for your loved ones. This whole wheat bread recipe, inspired by traditional Italian methods, is both nutritious and delicious. Let's dive into the world of bread-making!

Details:

- **Servings:** 8

- **Prep Time:** 50 minutes

- **Bake Time:** 60 minutes

Ingredients:

- 1 kg (roughly 8 cups) of whole wheat flour

- 130g (a smidge under ½ cup) of unrefreshed sourdough starter

- 650 ml (a tad over 2¾ cups) of water

- 18g (around 1 tablespoon) of salt

- 45g (3 tablespoons) of wheat germ (this is optional, but it's a great touch for added nutrition)

Let's Get Baking:

1. **The Sourdough Spa Treatment:** We're using our sourdough starter straight-up, no refresh. But first, it gets a little pampering. Soak it in lukewarm water (that's about 82.4°F) with a couple of teaspoons of sugar. This 30-minute soak helps mellow out the acidity, making for a smoother dough and a tastier bread.

2. **Kneading Time:** In a big bowl, mix together your flour, the pampered sourdough, water (aim for around 75°F), and any other ingredients you're using. If you've got wheat germ, toss it in now. Knead until everything's combined and you've got a nice, elastic dough.

3. **The Rise of the Dough:** Cover your dough and let it have a good long rest at room temperature. We're talking about 4 hours. This is its time to shine (or rise).

4. **Shape Up:** Post-rise, it's time to shape your dough into loaves. Pop each one into a floured basket or mold. Cover them up with a clean cloth and let them chill in the fridge for 10-12 hours.

5. **Oven Time:** Before you pop them in the oven, give your loaves a little character by making some incisions on top. Preheat your oven and create a steamy environment with a pot of boiling water. This helps the bread get that lovely crust. Bake at 392°F. A few minutes in, remove the water and crack the oven door to let the bread dry a bit.

6. **Enjoy:** And there you have it! A loaf of rustic, hearty whole wheat bread that'll transport you straight to the Italian countryside. Store any leftovers in a food-grade bag, and they'll stay fresh for up to a week.

Happy baking and buon appetito!

Ah, the joy of baking! Dive into the world of Italian bread-making with these Ciabatta Slippers. Their name might sound quirky, but their taste is all about that classic Italian crunch and aroma. Perfect for sandwiches or just a dab of butter.

Let's get started!

Details:

- **Servings:** 2

- **Prep Time:** 20 minutes

- **Bake Time:** 35 minutes

For the Poolish (a type of starter):

- 160g (about ⅔ cup) of licoli (or if you have it, 100g or a little less than ½ cup of sourdough starter)

- 75g (roughly ⅔ cup) of all-purpose flour (flour 0 in Italy)

- 65g (about ¼ cup) of water

For the Main Dough:

- 325g (around 2¾ cups) of all-purpose flour

- 190g (close to ¾ cup) of water

- 9g (about 1½ teaspoons) of salt

Baking Steps:

1. **The Flour Matters:** For this recipe, we're looking for a flour that's thirsty – it should be able to soak up a good amount of water.

2. **Poolish Time:** Whip up your poolish using the ingredients listed above. Once mixed, cover it with some plastic wrap and let it dream of becoming bread overnight at room temperature.

3. **Dough Day:** The next morning, your poolish is ready to roll. Toss it into a mixer or a big bowl, add in the water, flour, and salt from the main dough ingredients, and get kneading.

4. **Rest and Rise:** Transfer that lovely dough into an oiled baking dish. Cover it up with some foil and let it take a nap in an oven that's turned off but has the light on. This rest lasts about an hour.

5. **Fold it Up:** Every 30 minutes, give your dough some love with 4 sets of folds.

6. **Shape and Rise Again:** After its rest, bring the dough out onto a floured surface. Divide it in two and shape each half into that classic ciabatta rectangle. Lay them on a floured tea towel, cover, and let them rise for another hour and a half.

7. **Baking Magic:** Transfer your risen ciabattas onto a baking sheet lined with parchment paper. If you've got a steam oven, use it. If not, pop a small pot of boiling water into the oven to create some steam. Bake at a fiery 482°F for 20 minutes. After that, reduce the heat to 302°F, ditch the steam, and bake for another 15 minutes.

And there you have it! Crunchy, aromatic Ciabatta Slippers, fresh from your oven. Slice one open, take in that fresh-baked aroma, and enjoy the fruits of your labor. Buon appetito!

A Crispy Outside, Soft Inside Delight

Imagine walking through the bustling streets of Palermo, Sicily, and catching a whiff of freshly baked bread. That's the aroma of the Sicilian Muffuletta, a bread with a rich history and an even richer taste. Traditionally baked for the feast of the dead, this bread was once a gift to the departed, filled with olive oil, anchovies, oregano, and cheese. Today, it's a gift to our taste buds, perfect for sandwiches or simply enjoyed with some olive oil and seasonings.

Details:

- **Servings:** 8
- **Prep Time:** 10 minutes
- **Bake Time:** 20 minutes

Ingredients:

- 250g of manitoba flour (about 2 cups, similar to bread flour in the U.S.)
- 250g of durum wheat semolina (about 2 cups)
- Approximately 250ml of water (about 1 cup)
- 150g of sourdough starter (roughly ⅔ cup)
- 1 tablespoon of honey
- 30ml of olive oil (about 2 tablespoons)
- 10g of salt (approximately 2 teaspoons)
- Sesame seeds (for coating)

Let's Get Baking:

1. **Mixing the Basics:** In a large bowl, combine room temperature water, sourdough starter, and honey. Sift together the two flours and gradually mix them into the wet ingredients. If you're doing this by hand, channel your inner Italian nonna and knead with love.

2. **Getting the Texture Right:** Depending on your flours, you might need to adjust the water a bit. Aim for a soft dough that's not too sticky. Once you've got the right consistency, gradually mix in the olive oil, followed by the salt.

3. **First Rise:** Shape your dough into a ball, place it in a bowl, and cover it with plastic wrap. Let it rest and rise in a warm spot, like an oven with

just the light on. This should take about 3 hours, or until it's doubled in size.

4. **Shaping:** Once risen, bring out your dough and divide it into portions, about 3.5 oz each (or the size of a small apple). Shape each portion into a round loaf, folding the edges inward.

5. **Sesame Coating:** Brush the top of each loaf with water and dip it into sesame seeds for that classic crunchy top.

6. **Second Rise:** Place your sesame-coated loaves on a baking sheet and let them rise again until they've doubled in size.

7. **Baking Time:** Preheat your oven to 392°F. Place your loaves in the middle rack and bake for about 20 minutes. They should come out with a golden-brown hue.

8. **Cool and Enjoy:** Let them cool a bit before diving in. The outside will be crispy, but inside, you'll find a soft and fluffy texture.

Serving Suggestion: True to Sicilian tradition, drizzle your Muffuletta with fresh olive oil, sprinkle some anchovies, oregano, and grated cheese. Buon appetito!

Step into the world of Milanese baking with this iconic, star-shaped bread. Known for its airy crumb and crunchy crust, the Michetta is a versatile choice—equally delicious when hot and an excellent vessel for cold cuts and cheeses. Ready to get started?

Details:

• **Servings**: 4

• **Preparation Time**: 40 minutes

• **Cooking Time**: 25 minutes

For the Dough:

- **500g (about 4 cups) of Flour 0**: The foundation of your Michetta

- **150g (roughly ⅔ cup) of Sourdough**: The leavening agent

- **350ml (about 1½ cups) of Water**: The unifying element

- **2 teaspoons of Honey**: A hint of sweetness

- **1 teaspoon of Salt**: The seasoning

Baking Steps:

1. **Yeast Preparation**: Refresh your sourdough for 5-6 hours, ideally overnight, and place it in a planetary mixer.

2. **Initial Mixing**: Add water and honey to the mixer and start at a low speed.

3. **Incorporate Dry Ingredients**: Gradually add the flour and salt to the mix.

4. **Knead to Texture**: Continue kneading, upping the speed slightly until the dough is soft and elastic.

5. **Rest in Cold**: Shape the dough, place it in a bowl, cover with foil, and refrigerate for 24 hours.

6. **Temperature Adjustment**: Remove the dough from the fridge and allow it to come to room temperature for an hour.

7. **First Fold**: Roll out the dough and make three folds. Cover with a tea towel and let it rest for an hour.

8. **Second Fold**: Repeat the folding and resting process.

9. **Shape and Oil**: Roll out the dough into a rectangle, fold it, and lightly coat with olive oil. Rest for 30 minutes.

10. **Portion the Dough**: Cut into 90g loaves. Hand-press and make three folds on each.

11. **Michetta Shaping**: Flatten the loaves with a rolling pin and cut strips to roll them up. Use an apple cutter to achieve the Michetta's signature shape. Rest for 2 hours.

12. **Baking Time**: Preheat your oven to 250°C. Place the Michettas on a baking sheet, dust with semolina flour, and bake for 25 minutes.

13. **Steam Technique**: For optimal crust, place a small pot of water in the lower part of the oven during baking.

Your Michettas are now ready to grace your table, capturing the essence of Milan in every bite. Whether you enjoy them fresh out of the oven or as the base for a sumptuous sandwich, they're a treat for the senses. Buon appetito!

Let's delve into crafting the iconic French Baguette—a bread that transcends mere sustenance to become a symbol of French culture. With its signature crispy crust and fluffy interior, this baguette is the ideal companion for your morning brew or a filling sandwich.

Details:

- **Servings:** Yields 1 Baguette

- **Preparation Time:** 40 minutes

- **Cooking Time:** 40 minutes

Ingredients for the Dough:

- 500g (roughly 4 cups) all-purpose flour

- 350ml (approximately 1.5 cups) water

- 7g (around 1.5 teaspoons) active dry yeast

- 10g (close to 1.75 teaspoons) salt

Baking Steps:

1. **Initial Blend**: In a spacious mixing bowl, blend 500g of all-purpose flour with 350ml of water. Stir until just combined, then add 7g of active dry yeast.

2. **Kneading Phase**: Work the dough for a solid 10 minutes, then fold in 10g of salt. Continue kneading for an additional 10 minutes.

3. **First Rise**: Shield the dough with a moist cloth and let it ascend for 2 hours. Post-rise, mold the dough and allow another 2-hour rise. This step is to be repeated thrice.

4. **Shaping**: Carefully move the dough to a floured countertop. Shape it into an elongated oval.

5. **Final Form**: Transform the oval dough into a cylinder measuring 18 inches in length.

6. **Preparation for Baking**: Position the cylindrical dough on a parchment-lined and lightly floured baking sheet. Envelop it with plastic wrap and let it rest for a quarter of an hour.

7. **Cold Fermentation**: To deepen the flavors, refrigerate the dough for 9-10 hours.

8. **Final Rise**: Take the dough out of the fridge and allow a room-temperature rise for one more hour.

9. **Pre-Baking Ritual**: Mist the dough lightly with water and carve diagonal slits using a razor-sharp knife or box cutter.

10. **The Bake**: Heat your oven to 464°F (240°C). Bake your masterpiece for about 40 minutes, or until it achieves a golden-brown hue.

Your French Baguette is now a reality, ready to elevate any meal or moment. Enjoy it hot from the oven or as the base of a scrumptious sandwich. Bon appétit!

Indulge in the soft and versatile Arabian Bread, a culinary gem with Turkish roots.

Similar in texture to piadina or tortillas, this bread can be made with or without yeast and serves as the perfect base for a incredible variety of dishes.

Details:

- **Servings**: Yields 6 pieces

- **Preparation Time**: 30 minutes

- **Cooking Time**: 15 minutes

Ingredients:

- 300g (about 2.5 cups) durum wheat semolina, rimacinata

- 100g (about 1/2 cup) sourdough starter, refreshed

- 150ml (approximately 2/3 cup) lukewarm water

- 1/2 teaspoon honey or sugar

- 1/2 teaspoon fine salt

Baking Steps:

1. **Initial Blend**: In a bowl, dissolve the sourdough starter with lukewarm water and honey (or sugar).

2. **Flour Incorporation**: Add the durum wheat semolina to the liquid mixture, followed by the salt.

3. **Kneading**: Work the dough until it becomes smooth and elastic. If you're using a stand mixer, knead for about 5 minutes.

4. **First Rise**: Allow the dough to rise in a warm, draft-free area for 3 hours. After this period, divide the dough into three equal parts.

5. **Shaping**: Use your hands to shape each portion into a round, flat loaf. Aim for about an inch in thickness to ensure the bread forms its characteristic inner pocket.

6. **Preparation for Baking**: Line a baking sheet with parchment paper and sprinkle it with some semolina. Place the shaped loaves on the sheet and sprinkle more semolina on top.

7. **Final Rise**: Cover the loaves with dampened parchment paper (well-wrung out) and let them rest for another 2 hours at room temperature.

8. **The Bake**: Preheat your oven to 392°F (200°C). Bake the bread for 15 minutes in a static oven.

9. **Multi-Pan Baking**: If you're baking more than one pan, switch to a convection oven setting for more uniform cooking.

Your Arabian Bread is now ready to be enjoyed! Whether you use it as a wrap for grilled meats or simply savor it with some olive oil and za'atar, it's a treat for the senses.

These oil buns are the perfect sidekick to any meal or a tasty snack for kids.
They're versatile enough to be filled with either savory or sweet fillings—think
hazelnut cream or even a slice of cheese. The secret ingredient? A good-quality
extra virgin olive oil that adds a unique aroma and flavor.

Details:

- **Servings**: Makes 10 buns

- **Prep Time**: 40 minutes

- **Cook Time**: 15 minutes

Ingredients:

- 150g (about 2/3 cup) refreshed sourdough starter
- 500g (about 4 cups) all-purpose flour
- 300g (about 1 and 1/4 cups) water
- 2 tsp salt
- 1 tsp sugar
- 50g (about 1/4 cup) extra virgin olive oil
- Extra olive oil for folding

Instructions:

1. **Start the Dough**: In a large mixing bowl, combine the flour, half of the water, and the olive oil.

2. **Add the Starter**: Crumble in the refreshed sourdough starter, a bit at a time, while kneading at a slow pace.

3. **Season**: Incorporate the salt and sugar, followed by the remaining water.

4. **Knead**: Continue to knead until the dough is smooth, elastic, and not sticky.

5. **First Rise**: Transfer the dough to an oiled bowl, cover with plastic wrap, and let it rise until it doubles in size.

6. **Shape the Buns**: Once risen, divide the dough into 100g portions. Roll them out and lightly coat with extra virgin olive oil.

7. **Second Rise**: Place the shaped buns on a parchment-lined baking sheet. Cover and let them rise again until doubled in size, approximately 2 hours.

8. **Preheat and Bake**: Preheat your oven to 200°C (about 392°F). Before popping them in, brush the buns with some more olive oil. Bake for about 15 minutes until golden brown.

9. **Optional**: For an extra shine, you can brush the buns with a beaten egg before baking.

Enjoy your homemade oil buns, perfect for any occasion!

These rolls are comfort food at its finest, with a soft, fluffy texture and a subtle sweetness from the milk and sugar. The butter enriches the dough, giving it a lush, velvety quality that's irresistible.

The Details:

- **Servings:** Makes 8 rolls

- **Prep Time:** 50 minutes

- **Bake Time:** 60 minutes

Ingredients:

- 300g (about 1 and 1/4 cups) flour (W 260) *(Cake Flour or Pastry Flour equivalent)*

- 1.2kg (around 10 cups) Farina Tipo 1 *(High Gluten Flour equivalent)*

- 120g (about 1/2 cup) sourdough starter

- 20g (around 1 and 1/2 tablespoons) sugar

- 350g (close to 1 and 1/2 cups) milk

- 50g (almost 3 and 1/2 tablespoons) butter

- 9g (around 1 and 1/2 teaspoons) salt

Steps to Perfection:

1. **Start the Dough:** Pour 300 grams of milk into your mixing bowl.

2. **Add the Basics:** Blend in the yeast, sugar, and both types of flour. Begin kneading the mixture.

3. **Flavor and Texture:** A couple minutes into kneading, introduce the salt and butter.

4. **Smooth it Out:** Keep kneading until the dough is smooth, elastic, and perfectly blended.

5. **First Rise:** Take the dough out of the bowl, shape it into a round, and place it in a sealed container. Let it rest in a warm area for about 3 hours or until it doubles in size.

6. **Divide and Conquer:** Turn the dough onto a flat surface and cut it into 50g pieces. Lightly knead each piece with your fingers.

7. **Shape Up:** Roll each piece of dough back onto itself, then roll it in the opposite direction to create a tight, neat roll.

8. **Second Rise:** Place the shaped rolls on a baking sheet lined with parchment paper. Cover them and let rise until doubled in size, about 2 more hours.

9. **Preheat and Prep:** Preheat your oven to 356°F (180°C). Gently brush the roll tops with leftover milk.

10. **Time to Bake:** Slide the rolls into the oven and bake for about 20 minutes, or until beautifully golden brown.

Your Milk Bread Rolls are now ready for the spotlight. Whether enjoyed fresh and warm from the oven or used as the base for a delicious sandwich, you're in for a treat.

Enjoy!

Tuscan bread is a culinary paradox—deliciously simple yet complex in flavor. Its salt-free nature makes it the perfect companion for charcuterie, cheeses, and hearty soups.

This is slow food at its finest, offering a subtle tang that tantalizes the palate.

The Details:

- **Servings**: Serves 4
- **Prep Time**: 15 minutes
- **Bake Time**: 45 minutes

The Ingredients:

- 400g (roughly 1 and 3/4 cups) of refreshed sourdough starter
- 1kg (around 8 and 1/3 cups) of type 0 flour (Bread Flour equivalent)
- 500g (about 2 cups) of water

Steps to Culinary Bliss:

1. **The Foundation**: In your mixer's bowl, unite the sourdough starter, flour, and half of the warm water.

2. **The Kneading Dance**: Employ the dough hook at a gentle speed, gradually incorporating the remaining water. Continue until the dough achieves a smooth, uniform, and elastic texture.

3. **Mind the Time**: Limit your kneading to no more than 15 minutes. The delicate nature of type 0 flour can't withstand prolonged manipulation.

4. **Rest and Relax**: Allow the dough to unwind in an oil-greased bowl for approximately 30 minutes. Following the rest, divide it into four equal portions.

5. **Shape Your Destiny**: Craft your Tuscan loaves by rolling each portion onto itself, tapering the ends ever so slightly.

6. **The Rise**: Position the shaped loaves on a well-floured tea towel, seam-side up, in a warm and draft-free sanctuary. Await their majestic rise to double the original volume.

7. **The Final Act**: Preheat your oven to 392°F (200°C). Gently transfer the loaves onto a parchment-lined baking sheet or a baking stone. Bake for about 45 minutes, or until they sport a golden hue and yield a hollow sound upon tapping.

Your Timeless Tuscan Bread is now ready to grace your table. Whether you're pairing it with a sumptuous cheese board or a comforting bowl of soup, you're in for an authentic Italian experience. Buon appetito!

Hamburger buns are an American culinary icon, yet their irresistible softness and rich flavor have captivated taste buds worldwide. These buns are the unsung heroes that elevate any burger from good to unforgettable.

The Details:

- **Servings**: Makes 6 buns

- **Prep Time**: 40 minutes

- **Bake Time**: 40 minutes

Ingredients:

- 150g (about 1 and 1/4 cups) of flour 00 *(Cake Flour or Pastry Flour equivalent)*

- 150g (about 1 and 1/4 cups) of Manitoba flour *(High Protein Bread Flour or Strong Bread Flour equivalent)*

- 150g (roughly 2/3 cup) of refreshed mother yeast

- 180ml (around 3/4 cup) of lukewarm water

- 20g (approximately 1 1/2 tablespoons) of sugar

- 30g (nearly 2 tablespoons) of soft butter

- 20g (around 1 1/2 teaspoons) of salt

- 1 egg (plus an additional one for brushing)

- Sesame seeds for garnish

Steps to Burger Bliss:

1. **The Perfect Blend**: Combine all the ingredients to form a supple, cohesive dough.

2. **The Waiting Game**: Cover the dough with a pristine tea towel and let it rise in a warm spot for at least 4 hours, or until it has doubled in volume.

3. **Portion Control**: Divide the dough into six evenly weighted segments.

4. **Shape and Place**: Grease your baking dish and form 2-3 cm high discs from each dough portion.

5. **Second Rise**: Cover the shaped buns and let them rest for another 90 minutes.

6. **The Finishing Touch**: Once the buns have risen beautifully, brush them with a beaten egg and sprinkle with sesame seeds.

7. **Golden Glory**: Bake in a preheated 356°F (180°C) oven for 15-20 minutes, or until they achieve a luscious golden-brown hue.

Storage Tips:

Your freshly baked buns can be stored in a plastic bag in the refrigerator for up to 2-3 days, or you can freeze them for future burger endeavors.

Your Classic American Hamburger Buns are now ready to take any burger to the next level. Whether it's a classic beef patty or a plant-based marvel, these buns are the perfect vessel. Enjoy!

Cassette Bread is not just a loaf; it's an experience. Its texture is a harmonious blend of softness and chewiness, while the subtle interplay of honey and butter creates a flavor profile that is nothing short of poetic.

The Specifics:

- **Servings**: Yields 4 Loaves

- **Preparation Time**: A mere 90 minutes

- **Baking Time**: 40 minutes of olfactory delight

The Components:

- 100g (approximately 1/2 cup) of invigorated sourdough starter

- 300g (around 2 1/2 cups) of Manitoba flour, the baker's choice

- 50ml (just over 3 tablespoons) of water, tepid

- 100ml (a scant 1/2 cup) of milk, preferably whole

- 35g (close to 2 1/2 tablespoons) of unsalted butter

- 1 teaspoon of sea salt, finely ground

- 1 teaspoon of organic honey

The Journey to Perfection:

1. **Awakening the Starter**: Gently dissolve your refreshed sourdough starter in warm water.

2. **The Alchemy**: Introduce the flour, milk, butter, salt, and honey into the mix. The magic begins here.

3. **The Art of Kneading**: Engage with the dough for 15 minutes, let it rest as if taking a short nap for 10 minutes, and then re-engage for another 10 minutes.

4. **The Repose**: Fashion the dough into a spherical shape, place it in a bowl, and swaddle it in plastic wrap.

5. **The Ascent**: Allow the dough to ascend in volume for about 2 hours in a warm, undisturbed location.

6. **The Sculpt**: Unveil the dough onto a flat canvas and roll it into itself, as if it were a scroll containing ancient secrets.

7. **The Final Proof**: Nestle the scroll-like loaf into a parchment-lined loaf pan and place it in an oven with only the light on—a warm, glowing cocoon.

8. **The Culmination**: Once the loaf has blossomed to twice its original volume, remove the parchment, ignite the oven to 356°F (180°C), and let it bake to a golden-brown nirvana for 35-40 minutes.

9. **The Denouement**: Allow the loaf its well-deserved rest before you slice into its tender crumb.

Preservation and Indulgence:

This loaf has the resilience of fine wine. Slice and freeze to ensure that you always have access to bread that is both fragrant and supple.

Your Cassette Bread is now a masterpiece, ready to elevate any meal or stand alone as a slice of pure bliss. Bon appétit!

Savory Pan Brioche offers a homemade, nutritious alternative to store-bought bread, and it's filled with delicious ingredients like Hungarian salami and Emmenthal cheese. It's perfect as an appetizer or even as a main course when paired with a side of vegetables.

Details:

- **Portions**: Makes 2 large braids

- **Preparation Time**: 10 minutes

- **Cooking Time**: 30 minutes

Ingredients for the Savory Brioche Dough:

- 150g (about 1/2 cup) sourdough starter

- 150g (about 1 cup) flour

- 40g (about 3 tablespoons) milk

- 1 teaspoon sugar

- 1 egg

- 40g (about 3 tablespoons) butter

- 1 teaspoon salt

For the Stuffing:

- Hungarian salami

- Spreadable cheese

- Emmenthal cheese

Instructions:

1. **Prep the Yeast**: Refresh the sourdough starter the night before you plan to use it.

2. **Initial Mix**: Dissolve the sourdough starter in warm milk and add sugar. Stir until smooth.

3. **Incorporate Flour**: Add some sifted flour to the mixture and allow it to absorb.

4. **Add Butter**: Incorporate soft butter and let it fully absorb into the mixture.

5. **Egg and Salt**: Add a beaten egg with a pinch of salt and knead until the dough is well-blended. Then, add the remaining flour.

6. **Hand Kneading**: Knead by hand for an additional 5 minutes and shape the dough into a ball.

7. **First Rise**: Place the dough in a covered container and let it rise for 2-3 hours in an oven turned off but with the light on, aiming for a temperature of 26-28°C (82.4°F).

8. **Shape and Stuff**: Roll out the dough on a lightly floured surface into a rectangle. Spread your choice of cheese, add slices of Hungarian salami, and top with slices of Emmenthal.

9. **Roll and Seal**: Roll up the dough tightly and seal the edges.

10. **Second Rise**: Place the roll on a baking sheet lined with parchment paper and let it rise again in the turned-off oven for 3-4 hours.

11. **Preheat and Prep**: Preheat your oven. Brush the surface of the roll with a bit of milk and sprinkle with seeds like sunflower, flax, or sesame.

12. **Bake**: Place in the oven and bake at 356°F (180°C) for about 25-30 minutes.

13. **Cool and Serve**: Allow the savory brioche to cool before slicing.

This Savory Pan Brioche is perfect as an appetizer or as a main course when accompanied by a hearty plate of vegetables. Enjoy!

Imagine waking up to the smell of freshly baked brioche wafting through the air. It's like a warm hug for your senses. This isn't just bread; it's a moment of pure joy, captured in a recipe. So, let's get baking!

Details:

- **Yields**: 2 beautiful braids

- **Prep Time**: A quick 10 minutes

- **Bake Time**: 30 minutes of heavenly aroma

What You'll Need:

- 150g of your best sourdough starter, refreshed and ready

- A spoonful of honey, for that touch of sweetness

- 180ml of milk, make it whole for extra richness

- 400g of flour, half 00 and half Manitoba, because why settle?

- 130g of sugar, the sweeter the better

- 100g of butter, unsalted and melted

- 1 egg, beaten

- A pinch of salt, about 5g should do

Let's Make Magic:

1. **The Starter**: In your mixer, blend the sourdough, warm milk, and honey until it's as smooth as a Sinatra song.

2. **Flour Power**: Sift your flours and add them slowly, like you're sprinkling fairy dust.

3. **Sweeten Up**: Time for sugar! Add it in and let the mixer do its thing.

4. **The Richness**: Drop in the beaten egg and melted butter. Take it slow; we're crafting art here.

5. **Last Touches**: Add the remaining flour and a pinch of salt. Keep kneading until your dough is as smooth as a baby's bottom.

6. **Rest and Relax**: Let the dough chill in the mixer for about 15 minutes. It's been through a lot.

7. **Fold It Like a Pro**: Take out the dough and give it some good old-fashioned 3-way folds. Then, shape it into a ball.

8. **The Rise of the Dough**: Cover it up and let it rise in a warm spot. You're aiming for it to double in size, which should take around 3-4 hours.

9. **Braid and Wait**: Divide the dough into three and braid it like you're weaving dreams. Cut it in half, seal the ends, and let it rise again. Yes, patience is key.

10. **The Grand Finale**: Preheat your oven to 170°C. Give the braid a gentle milk wash if you like, and then bake it for 30 minutes.

And there you have it! Your Sweet Brioche Rolls are ready to steal the show. Whether you're enjoying them fresh out of the oven or saving them for later, they're a slice of heaven. Enjoy!

Let's talk about the final flourish in bread-making: decoration.

This is where culinary skill meets artistry, where you get to put your personal stamp on your homemade loaf. It's not just about how your bread tastes, but also how it looks when it finally comes out of the oven.

So, let's dive into the techniques that will make your bread as beautiful as it is delicious.

Essentials for the Job:

- A razor-sharp blade, akin to what a barber would use.

- Flour for dusting

- A small sieve

- Optional: A stencil for specialized designs

Step-by-Step Guide:

1. **Ready for the Spotlight**: Ensure your bread dough has doubled in size and looks almost oven-ready.

2. **Snowfall on Bread Mountain**: Fill your small sieve with flour and sprinkle it generously over the loaf, as if you're dusting powdered sugar on a cake.

3. **Feather-Light Fingers**: Gently massage the flour into the bread's surface. The key word here is 'gentle'; you don't want to deflate your beautiful loaf.

4. **The Creative Phase**: With your razor blade, make swift, shallow cuts for decorative purposes and deeper, 1 cm cuts for the bread's structural integrity.

5. **Patience Pays Off**: Unlike my initial attempt where I rushed the bread into the oven, wait for about 5-7 minutes after making your cuts before baking.

6. **Last-Minute Adjustments**: Right before it goes into the oven, retrace the deeper cuts to ensure they are sufficiently deep.

7. **Baking Time**: Place your artfully decorated loaf into a preheated oven and bake as usual.

Expert Tips:

- **Precision Matters**: The thinner the blade, the more intricate and appealing your decorations will be.

- **Stencil Sophistication**: If you're looking to add a touch of complexity, use a stencil. Position it over the dough, sprinkle flour through it, and carefully lift it off.

And there you go! Your bread is now a visual masterpiece, ready to wow anyone who lays eyes on it. Enjoy the process and the delicious results!

PIZZA

This sourdough pizza recipe offers a delightful blend of flavors and is gentle on the stomach.

While the preparation is straightforward, it's essential to start kneading the dough the evening before you plan to bake.

This allows the sourdough to rejuvenate properly. Once that's done, simply follow the detailed steps to craft your pizza.

You'll be rewarded with a pie that boasts an enchanting medley of aromas and textures.

Italian Pizza

Dive into the heart of Italy with this authentic Italian Pizza recipe.

A dish that has won hearts worldwide, this pizza promises a delightful blend of flavors and textures.

Crafted with love and tradition, every bite transports you to the cobbled streets of Naples, where pizza is not just food but an emotion.

Let's embark on this culinary journey and create a masterpiece that's both delicious and soul-satisfying.

Servings: 2

Preparation time: 30 min.

Cooking time: 15/20 min.

Ingredients:

- 300 gr (approximately 2 and 1/2 cups) flour 0 (Bread Flour equivalent)
- 300 gr (approximately 2 and 1/2 cups) flour 00 (Cake Flour or Pastry Flour equivalent)
- 200 gr (roughly 1 cup) sourdough
- 350 ml (around 1 and 1/2 cups) water
- Extra virgin olive oil
- 16 gr (around 2 and 2/3 teaspoons) fine salt
- Tomato puree
- Mozzarella
- Fresh basil

Instructions:

1. Refresh the sourdough the night before.

2. Come morning, dissolve the sourdough in room temperature water.

3. Gradually add both flours, kneading to achieve a smooth mix.

4. Incorporate the oil and salt, continuing to knead until the dough is firm and non-sticky.

5. Shape into a ball, cover, and let it rise in a warm spot for 4-5 hours or until doubled.

6. Transfer the risen dough to a floured surface and divide into two.

7. Hand-shape the pizzas, avoiding the use of a rolling pin and ensuring no air bubbles form.

8. Place on oiled baking sheets, cover, and allow a second rise.

9. Once risen, top with your preferred ingredients.

10. Bake in a preheated oven at 250°C (482°F) for 15-20 minutes.

Tips:

- For a room temperature rise, allow about 12 hours.

- For a longer fermentation, refrigerate the dough for 48 hours, taking it out 60-90 minutes before shaping.

- If opting for extended fermentation, fold the dough a second time an hour after the initial fold.

- For baking, use a refractory stone if available. Shape the dough Neapolitan-style with thicker edges.

- Add mozzarella 3-4 minutes before the end of baking to prevent burning.

- Preheat the oven and stone (if using) to 250°C (482°F) and monitor the pizza during baking.

With this recipe in hand, you're all set to recreate the magic of Italian pizzerias in your own kitchen. Buon appetito!

Focaccia

Experience the heart of Italy with this traditional focaccia recipe. With its crispy exterior and soft interior, infused with the rich aroma of olive oil, this bread is reminiscent of Italian families gathering around their dining tables. Let's embark on this culinary journey together.

Servings: 5

Preparation Time: 45 minutes

Cooking Time: 30 minutes

Ingredients:

- 500 gr flour (type 0) (about 4 cups of all-purpose flour)

- 180 gr (about 3/4 cup) refreshed sourdough starter

- 350 gr (about 1 1/2 cups) room temperature water

- 50 ml (about 3 1/2 tablespoons) extra virgin olive oil

- 1 teaspoon of honey or sugar

- 10 gr (about 1 3/4 teaspoons) salt

- *Emulsion:* 40 gr (about 3 tablespoons) olive oil, 40 gr (about 3 tablespoons) water, and a pinch of salt

Instructions:

1. Begin by refreshing 180 gr of sourdough starter, allowing it to rest for several hours.

2. In a mixing bowl, combine the sourdough, water, and honey, stirring until nearly dissolved.

3. Gradually add the flour and oil, ensuring the flour is fully incorporated.

4. Introduce the salt and continue mixing.

5. Transfer your dough to a sizable bowl, covering it with plastic wrap. Allow it to rise for 8-10 hours.

6. Once risen, move the dough to an olive oil-greased baking dish.

7. Gently spread the dough to fill the dish and let it rest for an additional hour.

8. Use your fingers to create dimples on the focaccia's surface. Generously drizzle with the prepared emulsion.

9. Finish with a sprinkle of coarse salt (and optionally, rosemary).

10. Bake in an oven preheated to 392°F (200°C) for roughly 30 minutes, or until a golden hue is achieved.

11. After baking, allow the focaccia to cool slightly before indulging.

Note: To ensure optimal fermentation, never add salt directly to the flour.

Savor the taste of Italy with every bite of your homemade focaccia!

Dive into the rich culinary heritage of Lazio with Pala Romana, a distinctive oval-shaped pizza that has won the hearts of Italians nationwide. The name "Pala Romana" traces its roots to the Latin term "pinsare," which translates to "to press" or "to crush." This is a nod to its unique hand-stretched formation, ensuring a crust that's both crispy and airy.

Servings: 2

Preparation Time: 25 minutes

Cooking Time: 8 minutes

Ingredients:

- 400 gr (about 3 1/3 cups) of type 00 flour (220/380W)
- 75 gr (about 2/3 cup) of rice flour

- 25 gr (about 1/4 cup) of soy flour

- 400 gr (about 1 3/4 cups) of cold water

- 100 gr (about 1/2 cup) of sourdough or licoli

- 3 gr (about 1/2 teaspoon) of malt (optional)

- 15 gr (about 2 1/2 teaspoons) of salt

- 20 gr (about 1 1/2 tablespoons) of EVO oil

Instructions:

1. Begin by sifting the flours. Combine them with half the water, either in a mixer with a paddle attachment on low speed or by hand.

2. Gradually incorporate the sourdough and malt.

3. Knead diligently for 15 minutes, ensuring the development of a robust gluten network.

4. Slowly introduce the remaining water, reserving a small portion for later stages.

5. Increase your kneading speed slightly.

6. Introduce the salt, enhancing the dough's elasticity.

7. Gradually fold in the oil, ensuring each addition is fully absorbed before proceeding.

8. Incorporate the reserved water.

9. Your dough should now exhibit a soft, creamy texture. Switch to a dough hook and knead for an additional 10-15 minutes.

10. Transfer the dough to an oil-greased container, covering it securely.

11. Allow it to rise until it doubles in size, which should take about 30-45 minutes.

12. Refrigerate the dough for a minimum of 24 hours.

13. Once removed from the fridge, let it sit at room temperature until it doubles in volume.

14. Generously flour your work surface with rice flour and turn out the dough.

15. Divide the dough in half, folding each portion into a cylindrical shape.

16. Rotate the dough 90° and fold again.

17. Shape the dough into its signature oval form.

18. Allow it to rest briefly until it rises slightly.

19. Flour your surface again with rice flour, placing the dough atop. Gently press the dough, ensuring you maintain its gas bubbles.

20. Shake off any excess flour.

21. Garnish with either tomato puree or a blend of water, salt, and EVO oil.

22. Preheat your oven to 482°F (250°C). Bake each pizza individually for 8-9 minutes if using a standard oven.

Note: The Pala Romana's charm lies in its delicate balance of flavors and textures. Its crispy crust, combined with the freshness of its toppings, offers a taste of Italy in every bite. Enjoy this Lazio specialty with your favorite toppings and a glass of Italian wine. Buon appetito!

Experience the magic of traditional Italian baking with this delightful recipe. These half-moon shaped delights, reminiscent of the Italian countryside, are a testament to the beauty of simplicity. Crafted with a blend of fine flours and the aromatic touch of EVO oil, these pockets of joy are perfect for any filling of your choice. Whether it's a savory treat or a sweet indulgence, these half-moons are sure to elevate your culinary experience.

Servings: 5

Preparation Time: 20 minutes

Cooking Time: 12 minutes

Ingredients:

- 450gr (about 3 3/4 cups) of type 00 flour (240/290W)

- 150gr (about 1 1/4 cups) durum wheat semolina

- 360g (about 1 1/2 cups) of water

- 150gr (about 2/3 cup) of refreshed sourdough or 100 of licoli

- 2.5gr (about 1/2 teaspoon) malt (optional)

- 18gr (about 3 teaspoons) salt

- 15gr (about 1 tablespoon) of EVO oil

Instructions:

1. Begin by combining water, flour, malt, and sourdough. Knead this mixture diligently for about 15 minutes.

2. As your kneading nears completion, gradually incorporate the salt and oil. Ensure a steady, continuous pour for a smooth blend.

3. Your dough should now exude a smooth, silky texture, indicative of its readiness.

4. Transfer the dough to a work surface, covering it with an inverted bowl. Allow it to rest for 30-45 minutes.

5. Divide the dough into 230gr portions. Shape each portion, employing the pirlatura technique for a refined texture.

6. Arrange these portions spaciously in a container.

7. Post-rise, flour your work surface and gently flatten each dough ball into delicate discs. Be cautious to preserve the air bubbles within.

8. Place your chosen fillings at the center of each disc. Fold the dough over the filling, sealing it into a half-moon shape.

9. Ensure a tight seal by pressing along the edges, reinforcing the closure.

10. Preheat your oven to 482°F (250°C) and bake these half-moons to perfection.

Note: The beauty of this recipe lies in its versatility. Feel free to experiment with fillings, from classic Italian ingredients to contemporary favorites. Whether it's a burst of mozzarella and tomato or a sweet chocolate and hazelnut spread, these half-moons are the perfect canvas for your culinary creativity. Buon appetito!

A staple of Italian tables and a beloved snack worldwide. These slender, crispy delights have graced many a meal, offering a crunchy contrast to soft cheeses and rich spreads. Whether you're sipping on a glass of wine or diving into a cheese platter, these breadsticks are the perfect companion.

Servings: 1

Preparation Time: 30 minutes

Cooking Time: 30 minutes

Ingredients:

- 200 gr (about 1 cup) of refreshed sourdough starter

- 200 gr (about 1 2/3 cups) of type 1 flour

- 100 ml (about 1/2 cup) lukewarm water

- 2 pinches of fine salt

- 2 tablespoons of extra virgin olive oil

- 3 tablespoons of grated parmesan cheese

- Sesame seeds for garnish

Instructions:

1. Begin by refreshing 200g of sourdough and allowing it to rise in a warm spot for several hours.

2. In a mixing bowl, dissolve the reactivated sourdough in warm water. Gradually add flour, salt, and oil.

3. Knead the mixture until you achieve a smooth, even dough.

4. Segment the dough into three equal portions. Retain two portions in their natural state, and blend the third with the grated parmesan cheese for an added flavor twist.

5. Break down the three dough segments into roughly 20-gram pieces. Roll each piece to craft the signature slender breadstick, ensuring a diameter of less than 1 cm.

6. For a touch of texture, sprinkle sesame seeds over the natural breadsticks. Press lightly to ensure they adhere.

7. Arrange the breadsticks on a baking tray lined with parchment paper. Allow them to rise for a few hours in a warm setting, such as an oven with only the light on.

8. Preheat your oven to 392°F (200°C). Bake the breadsticks for 20-30 minutes, or until they boast a golden hue and a crispy texture.

Serving Suggestions: These versatile breadsticks shine in their simplicity. Enjoy them as a standalone snack, or pair them with a range of accompaniments. From cold cuts and cheeses to jams and Nutella, these breadsticks are the perfect canvas for a host of flavors. Whether it's breakfast, an appetizer, or a midnight snack, they're always a delightful choice. Buon appetito!

Imagine a warm summer evening in Italy, the sun setting over the horizon, and a table set for a family dinner. Amidst the laughter and chatter, a dish stands out - the crispy, delicious friselle. These ring-shaped breads, reminiscent of doughnuts, are a staple in many Italian households during the summer months. Perfect for those impromptu gatherings with friends or a quick family dinner, friselle are the embodiment of simplicity and taste.

Servings: 4

Preparation Time: 30 minutes

Cooking Time: 25 minutes initial bake + 30 minutes secondary bake

Ingredients:

- 300 gr (about 1 1/3 cups) of sourdough starter, refreshed twice in 24 hours

- 300 gr (about 1 1/4 cups) of water

- 300 gr (about 2 1/2 cups) of semolina

- 300 gr (about 2 1/2 cups) of type 00 flour

- 10 gr (about 2 teaspoons) of extra virgin olive oil (EVO)

- 18 gr (about 3 teaspoons) of salt

Instructions:

1. Ensure the sourdough starter is refreshed twice within a 24-hour span.

2. Once the starter has risen adequately, segment the dough into individual portions, each weighing between 90 and 100 grams.

3. Shape each portion into sticks and then loop them to form ring-like structures, akin to doughnuts.

4. Arrange these rings on a baking tray lined with parchment paper, gently pressing them to flatten slightly.

5. Shield the dough with a clean kitchen towel and let them rise. For optimal results, place them in an oven with just the light on and a pot of hot water. This setup ensures the right humidity for the dough to rise.

6. Once risen, align them side by side on the baking tray, ensuring they don't overlap.

7. Bake in a preheated oven at 356°F (180°C) for about 20-30 minutes. The exact time might vary based on individual ovens.

8. After this initial bake, rearrange them on the tray and leave the oven door slightly ajar. Continue baking for an additional 30 minutes to achieve that perfect crispness.

Pro Tips:

- If the dough feels too dense or dry, feel free to add a couple of teaspoons of water to adjust the consistency.

- Once baked, friselle can be seasoned to your liking. A classic combination involves drizzling some salt, olive oil, fresh tomatoes, and a sprinkle of oregano. The result? A delightful crunch with a burst of Mediterranean flavors. Perfect for those summer nights!

Taralli

Imagine sitting in a quaint café in Apulia, Italy, with the warm sun gently touching your face. As you sip on a glass of local red wine, you reach out for a snack that's as traditional as the cobblestone streets of this region - the Taralli. These little ring-shaped wonders, often compared to bagels, have been a part of Apulian family recipes for generations. Their delightful crunch, combined with the aromatic hint of fennel seeds, makes them an irresistible treat.

Servings: 100

Preparation Time: 40 minutes

Cooking Time: 30 minutes

Ingredients:

- 120 gr of traditional sourdough starter

- 75 ml of fresh water

- 100 gr of durum wheat semolina

- 350 gr of flour 0 (akin to Bread Flour in the USA)

- 200 ml of water

- 50 ml of the finest extra virgin olive oil

- 25 ml of crisp white wine

- 1 tablespoon of aromatic fennel seeds

- A pinch of natural fine salt for that perfect seasoning

Steps to the Perfect Taralli:

1. Start by giving some love to your sourdough starter. Mix it with flour and knead until it feels like a soft loaf.

2. Cover this beauty with a tea towel, letting it rest and rise for an hour.

3. In a deep bowl, pour in the durum wheat semolina, the golden olive oil, and the white wine. This is where the magic starts - begin kneading.

4. As you feel the dough coming together, sprinkle in the salt and those fragrant fennel seeds.

5. Continue kneading until the dough feels smooth, like silk under your fingers. Shape it into a welcoming ball.

6. Let this ball of deliciousness rest in a bowl, away from any drafts, letting it rise until it's proudly doubled in size.

7. Once risen, lay the dough on a flat surface and gently knead. Break it into small pieces, each about 2 inches long.

8. Shape these pieces into rings, ensuring they overlap at the edges. Seal them with love and care.

9. Before these rings take their golden bath in the oven, give them a quick boil. Once drained, place them on a wire rack to rest.

10. Prepare your baking trays with parchment paper, placing the taralli in rows.

11. Bake them in a preheated oven at 347°F (175°C) until they wear a golden crown, which should be in about 30 minutes.

A Little Whisper from Apulia: Taralli can wear many hats. While some love them salted, others prefer the aromatic embrace of fennel seeds or the spicy kick of chili pepper. Whatever your heart desires, Taralli is here to please!

The savory pie is a celebration of flavors and textures, making it the star of buffets, picnics, and family gatherings. Whether you serve it as an appetizer or a main course, its layers of goodness are sure to impress.

Servings: Serves a hungry soul or a small gathering

Preparation Time: 45 minutes

Cooking Time: 30 minutes

Ingredients:

- 500 gr of semolina flour (a coarser grain that gives our pie a unique texture)

- 50 gr of freshly refreshed sourdough (for that perfect rise)

- 300 ml of water

- 2 teaspoons of salt (for that balanced flavor)

- 1 teaspoon of sugar (just a hint of sweetness)

- 2 tablespoons of the finest extra virgin olive oil

For the Heart of the Pie (Stuffing):

- 1 vibrant pepper

- 800 gr of hearty potatoes

- A drizzle of extra virgin olive oil

- A pinch of salt to season

Steps to Create the Perfect Savory Pie:

1. Begin by dissolving the refreshed sourdough in water. Add a touch of sugar.

2. In a mixing bowl or a planetary mixer, start at a low speed, gradually adding the flour and olive oil. As the ingredients come together, increase the speed.

3. Introduce the salt, dissolved in a splash of water, and continue kneading until the dough feels springy and elastic.

4. Shape this beauty into a ball and place it in a greased bowl. Cover it lovingly with plastic wrap and let it dream in the refrigerator overnight.

5. As dawn breaks, take the dough out and let it rise for another 4 hours, basking in the warmth of your kitchen.

6. While the dough rises, prepare the heart of your pie. Slice the peppers and potatoes and let them bathe in water. In a large skillet, heat some olive oil and introduce the peppers. After a few moments of sizzling, add the potatoes and season with salt. Let them dance together on low heat for about 30 minutes.

7. Once the dough has risen to its glory, divide it into two. Roll out each half, either by hand or with a rolling pin, feeling the texture under your fingers.

8. Grease your baking pan and lay down the first sheet of pastry. Gently spread the pepper and potato mixture over it, letting the flavors seep into the dough. Cover this with the second sheet, sealing the goodness within.

9. Bake this masterpiece in a preheated oven at 350°F. In about 30 minutes, it will turn a golden hue, signaling that it's ready to be devoured.

A Little Whisper from the Kitchen: The beauty of a savory pie lies in its versatility. Feel free to experiment with the stuffing - maybe some roasted veggies, or perhaps a sprinkle of cheese?

The canvas is yours to paint!

Mediterranean Whips

Embark on a culinary journey to the heart of the Mediterranean with these delightful whips. Crispy on the outside and soft on the inside, they capture the essence of Mediterranean cuisine. Perfect for dipping in olive oil, pairing with cheeses, or simply enjoying on their own, these whips are a testament to the simple pleasures of life.

Servings: Enough for a small gathering of 5

Preparation Time: 40 minutes

Cooking Time: 40 minutes

Ingredients:

- 500 gr of flour 0 (akin to Bread Flour in the USA)

- 10 gr of salt for that balanced flavor

- A touch of sweetness with 1 teaspoon of honey

- 35 gr of freshly refreshed sourdough, the heart of our whips

- 300 ml of pure, natural water

Steps to Craft the Perfect Mediterranean Whips:

1. Begin by placing the flour in a spacious bowl. Sprinkle the salt around the edges, creating a protective ring.

2. In the heart of this floury arena, add a dollop of honey.

3. In a separate vessel, dissolve the awakened sourdough in warm water, letting the two elements become one.

4. Gently pour this liquid mixture into the flour's center, where the honey awaits.

5. Dive in and start kneading, feeling the dough come alive under your fingers. Continue until it's springy and elastic.

6. Shape this mixture into a proud ball and let it rest, allowing it to rise and expand for about 3 hours.

7. Once risen, lay the dough on a floured canvas and knead it once more, pouring your love into every fold.

8. Divide this masterpiece into 5 equal portions. Shape each into an elongated whip, reminiscent of a slender baguette.

9. Place these whips on a baking sheet adorned with parchment paper. Dust them with a sprinkle of flour and let them rise for another hour, basking in anticipation.

10. With a gentle hand, make a delicate slanted incision atop each whip, adding character.

11. Preheat your oven to a toasty 200°C (392°F).

12. Slide the whips into the oven and let them bake for about 40 minutes. Once they turn a golden shade of perfection, they're ready to grace your table.

A Whisper from the Shores of the Mediterranean: These whips are versatile. Enjoy them fresh out of the oven, or toast slices to create the perfect bruschetta base. Drizzle with olive oil, top with fresh tomatoes, and sprinkle with basil for a bite of the Mediterranean.

Embark on a culinary journey to the heart of the Mediterranean with these delightful whips. Crispy on the outside and soft on the inside, they capture the essence of Mediterranean cuisine. Perfect for dipping in olive oil, pairing with cheeses, or simply enjoying on their own, these whips are a testament to the simple pleasures of life.

Servings: 5

Preparation Time: 40 minutes

Cooking Time: 40 minutes

Ingredients:

- 500 gr (approx. 4 cups) of flour 0 (akin to Bread Flour in the USA)
- 10 gr (approx. 2 teaspoons) salt
- 1 teaspoon honey for a hint of sweetness
- 35 gr (approx. 2.5 tablespoons) freshly refreshed sourdough
- 300 ml (approx. 1.25 cups) pure, natural water

Steps to Perfect Mediterranean Whips:

1. In a large mixing bowl, add the flour. Sprinkle the salt around its perimeter.
2. Create a well in the center and add the honey.
3. In a separate container, dissolve the sourdough in warm water.
4. Gradually pour this liquid mixture into the flour's center.
5. Begin kneading until the dough feels elastic and smooth.
6. Mold the dough into a ball and let it rise for about 3 hours.
7. Post rising, transfer the dough onto a floured surface.
8. Knead briefly and divide into 5 equal segments.
9. Shape each segment into an elongated whip, similar to a slender baguette.
10. Place them on a parchment-lined baking sheet, sprinkle with flour, and let them rise for an additional hour.
11. Gently make a slanted incision on each whip.
12. Preheat the oven to 200°C (392°F).
13. Bake for around 40 minutes until they achieve a golden hue.

Serving Suggestion: These whips are incredibly versatile. Enjoy them fresh, or toast slices to craft the ideal bruschetta. Drizzle with olive oil, top with fresh tomatoes, and a sprinkle of basil for a Mediterranean treat.

Indulge in the festive spirit with a homemade sourdough panettone. This traditional Italian treat, enriched with butter, eggs, and dried fruits, is a delightful centerpiece for any holiday table. Here's how you can craft this delicacy at home:

Servings: 1 panettone (approx. 1kg)

Preparation Time: 60 minutes

Cooking Time: 60 minutes

1st Dough Ingredients:

- 250 gr (approx. 2 cups) of Manitoba flour (akin to High Protein Bread Flour in the USA)

- 150 gr of refreshed sourdough starter from the previous day

- 130 gr (approx. 9 tablespoons) of butter

- 8 egg yolks

- 100 gr (approx. 1/2 cup) of sugar

- 80 gr (approx. 1/3 cup) of water

Aromatic Mix:

- 30 gr (approx. 2 tablespoons) of honey

- Grated zest of 1 lemon

- Grated zest of 1 orange

2nd Dough Ingredients:

- 80 gr (approx. 2/3 cup) of Manitoba flour (akin to High Protein Bread Flour in the USA)

- 90 gr (approx. 7/16 cup) of sugar

- 100 gr (approx. 7 tablespoons) of butter

- 150 gr (approx. 1 cup) of raisins

- 5 egg yolks

- 50 gr (approx. 1/3 cup) of candied orange peel

- 50 gr (approx. 1/3 cup) of candied citron

- Aromatic mix from above

- A pinch of salt

Instructions:

1. Refresh the yeast the day before making the panettone.

2. For the first dough, prepare a mixture of water and sugar, then add the flour until smooth and homogeneous.

3. Incorporate the egg yolks one by one, gradually.

4. Add the diced butter and sourdough mixture.

5. Mix the ingredients together and form a smooth, homogeneous ball that is stretchy when rolled.

6. Place in a bowl and let sit for at least 12 hours until it triples in volume.

7. Put 150g of raisins in water to soften.

8. Stir in the aromatic mixture and store in a sealed jar in the refrigerator.

9. For the second dough, melt the butter with the aromatics and let cool.

10. Take the previous day's dough and lay it out on a floured work surface.

11. Add flour, sugar, then incorporate egg yolks one by one and the aromatic mix.

12. Add the raisins. Let the dough rise in a bowl for 15 minutes.

13. Pour the dough into a foil-lined baking dish.

14. Let rise for 8 hours until the mixture reaches the edges of the bowl.

15. Bake the panettone for 1 hour at 320°F (160°C).

16. Insert a toothpick into the center of the panettone while it is baking to check if it is cooked.

17. Remove the panettone from the oven and pierce the bottom, going from side to side horizontally with 4 long skewers.

18. Leave to rest upside down for 12 hours.

Enjoy your homemade sourdough panettone!

Thank you deeply for your trust and for choosing our product. This manual is more than just a guide; it's a testament to the timeless art that we hold dear. My aspiration is for it to be a beacon, illuminating your path, enriching your skills, and deepening your appreciation for the craft. Your journey and dedication inspire us every day, and it's an honor to be a part of it. May this be the start of many masterpieces to come. Wishing you endless inspiration and success.

Warm regards,
Massimo Parrucci

(Please, if I have been helpful to you, leave a comment on Amazon)

Manufactured by Amazon.ca
Acheson, AB

13591271R00070